Jacqueline,

thanks for being
first, only, and friendliest
customer at Crystal Voyage . . . :

Best,

*[signature]*

It was wonderful speaking
with you. I will be interested
in finding and reading one
of your poems.

Heather

# LifeStorm

## The Prose and Prints

### Andy Tillo

*Bookman* LLC
Publishing & Marketing

*Providing Quality, Professional
Author Services*

www.BookmanMarketing.com

*"Don't live life regretting what you didn't do. Do what you might regret, otherwise, you'll never know..."*

# LifeStorm

**Andy Tillo**
**http://www.tillo13.com**

*Editor/Agent: VicToria Tallman Freudiger*
*www.digi-tall-news-media.com*

*Bookman Publishing & Marketing*
*Martinsville, Indiana*
*www.BookmanMarketing.com*

*{Cover Photograph taken by Andy Tillo}*

*Individual prints available for purchase at:*
*http://www.tillo13.com*

# Dedication

This book is dedicated to the one's who have touched my heart.
I thank you every day...

# Table of Contents

Prologue by VicToria
Introduction of the Author
Prologue by the Author

**I Wonder If She Knows -** *11/11/2003 11:09:00 AM*
**The Day I Died -** *2/2/2004 5:33:00 PM*
**Stuck On Cloud # 8 -** *2/11/2004 12:57:00 PM*
**Another Amazing Day -** *11/30/2003 9:11:00 AM*
**Starting Over -** *11/22/2003 10:42:00 AM*
**Your Choice -** *1/27/2004 11:39:00 AM*
**Coming Back Home -** *11/17/2003 5:22:00 PM*
**If You Wait For Me -** *11/6/2003 11:22:00 AM*
**Trying To Forget -** *9/25/2003 9:44:00 AM*
**Her Tears -** *10/28/2003 4:59:00 PM*
**Winning Her Heart -** *12/17/2003 10:32:00 AM*
**When You Come Back To Me -** *10/7/2003 5:04:00 PM*
**If I Had It To Do Over -** *10/6/2003 3:59:00 PM*
**Last Night -** *10/6/2003 3:37:00 PM*
**It's What I Wanted, Right? -** *10/3/2003 11:52:00 AM*
**Later -** *10/8/2003 11:24:00 AM*
**Falling In Love Again -** *10/2/2003 10:54:00 AM*
**Please Don't Stop -** *10/2/2003 10:30:00 AM*
**Permanent -** *9/25/2003 9:57:00 AM*
**As I Watched -** *10/17/2003 9:11:00 AM*
**Her Scent -** *10/15/2003 2:41:00 AM*
**My Angel -** *10/10/2003 4:41:00 PM*
**No Need To Reminisce -** *2/17/2004 5:52:00 PM*
**Burn The Town -** *2/13/2004 9:05:00 AM*

**Growing Up (Choices)** - *12/16/2003 9:10:00 AM*
**You Won** - *9/25/2003 9:58:00 AM*
**Little Things** - *2/10/2004 11:47:00 AM*
**It Might Be Love** - *2/9/2004 1:11:00 PM*
**Everyone Has Ghosts** - *2/5/2004 12:32:00 PM*
**The Blue Shoe Mystery** - *1/30/2004 11:10:00 AM*
**There Is A Place** - *1/23/2004 5:09:00 PM*
**If I Were You** - *1/22/2004 4:12:00 PM*
**I Have Lost You** - *9/26/2003 10:31:00 AM*
**Make The Night Last Longer** - *10/27/2003 3:49:00 PM*
**That Same Path** - *10/23/2003 8:40:00 AM*
**Always Been There For Me** - *10/21/2003 4:13:00 PM*
**Raining On Smilesville** - *10/21/2003 7:09:00 AM*
**To Be With You This Winter** - *10/20/2003 2:41:00 PM*
**Love's Counting On It** - *1/26/2004 3:09:00 PM*
**She Told Me** - *1/2/2004 9:22:00 AM*
**Take Me (At Her Bedside)** - *11/3/2003 1:06:00 PM*
**Did You Know I Watched You?** - *9/26/2003 11:44:00 AM*
**The Man I Am** - *9/26/2003 10:19:00 AM*
**I Forgot About You** - *9/25/2003 9:45:00 AM*
**You Stole My Heart** - *10/29/2003 11:33:00 AM*
**In Your Hands** - *10/2/2003 8:40:00 AM*
**You Make Me Smile Inside** - *10/1/2003 3:14:00 PM*
**To My Mother** - *9/29/2003 5:29:00 PM*
**I'm Struggling** - *12/29/2003 6:13:00 PM*
**Learning To Love Again** - *12/22/2003 5:23:00 PM*
**Gonna Be Cold Outside Tonight (At Least She Could Have Let Me Have The Couch!)** - *12/19/2003 11:10:00 AM*
**Never Around, But Always By Your Side** - *3/5/2004 12:30:00 PM*
**We Had A Chance** - *11/4/2003 10:04:00 AM*

**I Want To -** *3/3/2004 5:28:00 PM*
**When I Am Finally Laid To Rest -** *9/29/2003 10:40:00 AM*
**I Heard A Song Today -** *9/29/2003 9:55:00 AM*
**For Two Weeks -** *9/26/2003 12:42:00 PM*
**Shootin' Out the Stars -** *02/28/2003 2:02:00 PM*
**One More Guess -** *2/27/2004 5:31:00 PM*

# PROLOGUE
# By VicToria

My name is VicToria Tallman Freudiger and I am Editor-in-Chief of *Digi-Tall News & Media*, as well as being one of the poetry writers on AuthorsDen. On AuthorsDen.com, it is commonplace to read someone's poetry and then place comments about their written pieces where the author can read them. It is there, AuthorsDen.com, that I found Andy Tillo.

As an editor of poetry and a publisher of poetry books, it is natural for me to do more than read their poetry... I look at the possibilities of the poem being publishable. Andy's poetry caught my eye quickly. One night (during the latter part of 2003,) I simply sat back in my ergonomic chair and read and enjoyed his poetry for a couple of hours. In a short time, I found myself laughing, smiling to myself, and even at times, shedding a tear or two. It was easy to sense that Andy put his heart and soul into his writing.

"Always There For Me," was the poem written by Andy that caught my eye most. Quite a number of writers had left very positive comments for Andy about this poem. In reading these comments, it became easy for me to see that he was finding his way to the hearts of many writers on AuthorsDen. Therefore, I contacted him and encouraged him to publish his poetry in print format so that people other than just those who had Internet access would be able to enjoy his work also.

Andy was pleased that I was interested in publishing some of his poetry on our poetry website, Poetry Highway, located at http://www.poetryhighway.com. Our writer/agent relationship began in February 2004. When Andy and I signed a contract and at the time, my ability to enjoy his poetry, began increasing one hundred-fold. It has been a pleasure proofreading, editing and finally submitting these creative poems for publishing.

We are certain that you will enjoy the prints placed here within *LifeStorm*. Through this artistically wonderful endeavor, I too have been able to enjoy sights from around the world that I would never have seen had I not found Andy. We are certain as you familiarize yourself with his talent by reading his poetry and viewing his photographs that you will want to tell others about *LifeStorm*.

Now, without further ado, Andy and I present to you...mankind... his poetry, **LifeStorm** and his images of the world as he saw them.

> Learn to never give up on your dreams,
> Continue to hope for a better future, and
> Always believe in yourself.

# Introduction of the Author
## or quite simply,
## Biography of a Poet

I was born Andrew Thomas Tillo on March 22, 1979, to Debra and Thomas Tillo in Helena, Montana. Sports took up most of my time, especially baseball. My parents split-up when I was fourteen years old, and I stayed in Helena, with my mother.

I went through high school receiving exemplary marks in all subjects and excelling in baseball, which would later lead to my college decision.

When I became eighteen, I moved to Walla Walla, Washington in order to attend Whitman College. The passion that drove me there was baseball, but what kept me there, were the many friendships that I made, which I hope will last a lifetime. My Studio Art degree and creative imagination proved well to inspire me, as much of my inspiration and experiences were drawn from there. Some of my early poetry was written in Walla Walla, as my heart and mind were both motivated and captivated for four years.

After graduating from Whitman College, in May 2001, I took a job on a resort in the South Pacific. There I worked many different jobs, from lifeguard to showman. I left the South Pacific after the 9/11 tragedy. Tourism hit an all-time low; consequently, I headed off with four friends to live in Tokyo, Japan.

In Tokyo, I found a job working as a bartender from 6:00 p.m. to 7:00 a.m. nightly. My body could only take so much, so I ended up quitting after a brief stay. Nearing the end of my funds, I decided it was time to head back to the United States.

I chose to go back to Montana in order to live with my mother and younger brother Tanner. By helping them out around the house, I was able to provide more stability in the house.  In June of 2002, I left my job in Montana, and took off to Thailand.  For a month and one-half, I spent my time running up and down the Thai coastlines with a few friends.  We made many memories there, which I'm sure will never be forgotten.

Upon my return to the mainland, I moved in with several friends from college.  Here, I found a job at a company in the Seattle, Washington area.  I've been here for two years now and have not regretted the move at all.

I still travel extensively, when I am able to find the time.  I've visited India with my roommate, Akshay in January of 2003 and more recently, Africa with my friend, David.  Many of the prints from these travels are included in this work.

I feel that it is here, that I will stay for a while, as I have sights to move me, friends to inspire me, and many muses convincing me to continue my work...

# Prologue by the Author

*"Don't live life regretting what you didn't do. Instead, choose to do something that you might regret; otherwise, you'll never know what you could have regretted."*

Throughout life, I've had to make choices that have added to my development as a person. These choices did not simply create another set of choices to be made by me... they enhanced my life instead. It is my belief that people grow from their ideas and choices. Some of my choices were able to blossom with the results that I helped to create.

Another important reflection that I have had is that the impact a person has on another person is directly related to the amount of time and effort put forth by that person.

It is true. I have had many choices to make in my life. Some of the countless decisions that I have made actually ended up changing my life, some in a positive way, and some in a negative way. However, learning to deal with these choices, and accept the parts that I was unable to change, has led me to a better understanding of life.

I have also been shown that some things in life are meant to be the way that they are. For instance, loves are found, and loves are lost, some are never found again. Some things re-grow where they were taken away, and I learned that it was made that way for a reason.

Passion is built on these ideals, and realizing the effect that this can have on a person, will bring a better comprehension of what love is. Maybe it is about getting hurt; it wouldn't be called love, if there were no chance of being burned. That's where the passion can be found, and that is where I've recognized my best work was written, when it comes from my heart.

Never in my wildest dreams, would I ever have thought I'd have created so many heart-felt stories and thoughts, let alone, to be published.  Now, that I have started to share, and get feedback from the works, I believe that I am finally locating another stage in my life where I'm not putting my feelings behind someone that isn't real.  I'm placing my name to these works and the feelings that they provoke.  I'm also spreading these thoughts among the people that they're about, who've molded my life.

Each of my works has a specific person in my life that has created and sculpted the person that I am today, and I hope that they realize the impression that they've had on my life.

People, in the past, who saw my written works asked me why I hadn't shown them to a publisher.  At other times, I was asked, "What are you working on now?"  My reply was that there is a very specific group of people in this world that read poetry, and an even smaller group that write it, more so to share it.  Most people have something, somewhere, sometime that they have written and placed on a sheet of paper or on an old notebook.  Words of poetry maybe that they've never wanted to show anyone, but the influence that this could have on the person or place it's written about, could change a relationship or a string of relationships like you wouldn't even believe.

There is nothing wrong with keeping something like this hidden.  It's the choice of the writer; and the odds are, that it will never get found or repeated ever.  Nevertheless, maybe, at that exact moment, the author might have been molding a life by putting emotion to paper.  So many works in recent memory that I've read have related to what I've been feeling.  That's what many of my works bring out in people.  It's written specific to my ideals and emotions, but at the same time, I'm just a drop in the bucket, when you realize how many people there are in this world.

Billions of people each day, for hundreds of years, have the availability to read and relate to different works.  Yet, finding that specific author that is writing down that specific emotion is a chance in a lifetime coincidence. That piece of work, will be kept at heart to that person for the rest of their lives, comprehending that this same emotion has happened hundreds and hundreds of times; to the billions of people over a stretch of time.

Writing what I feel and believe in is an amazing thing to capture. My fulfilled goal is that I was able to, within these pages, relay these feelings and beliefs to my readers...

*Andy Tillo 2004*

# The
## Prose
### and
## Prints

# By Andy Tillo

# I Wonder If She Knows

*Tuesday, November 11, 2003*

Koh Phi Phi, Thailand – June 2002

I wonder if she knows,
the feelings, I have for her;
behind her back,
around our friends.

I think that I keep them hidden
well enough,
not to give it away,
yet.

The time is drawing near though,
when I won't be able to hold it back.
The words will flow,
from my lips,
hoping to find their way,
                    into her heart...

Managaha Island, Saipan, Northern Marianas – August 2001

# The Day I Died

*Wednesday, February 04, 2004*

*--To the best friend I ever had.*

Late November of 2001,
many hours of watching the setting sun,
I could hear the calls,
when all I had in me were quaint squalls.

Nothing left
in a body full of love;
I just couldn't let go of,
the person I thought most of.

Cold wind blew through my hair,

an icy stare
is all that was left there,
I could hardly move.
How badly I wanted to be home,
but my bones wouldn't budge
to make the trudge;
my head was spinning,
but this was only the beginning.
My blood was spilling
but I could still hear that voice
calling me home
when I had no choice
but to lie there in the snow.

Frosted Branches, Helena, Montana – December 2001

Ice slowly mixed its way into my veins;
throughout life, never so many pains,
in my legs and stomach,

but more in my heart;
as I firmly believed that I'd never
look into your beautiful eyes ever again,
from now to eternity.
I'd have to fight my way through the night;
drop to my knees and pray for morning light,
to help me into the arms of the one that made me
the most important part of their life.

As the night continued,
thoughts of us kept me alive.
Hoping that the sun would find me,
and your love would warm me.
I met you when I was so young,
I hardly remember it well,
but the memories made then
live long in my head again,
praying to make more memories
when I come to and feel your soft hand.

This morning, the sun won't break through
all that the sky brings is more snow.
God, please let my love sense it, let her know
I really didn't mean to let it all go;
but my face is cold, and
my heart is faded,
I tried to be bold,
and keep hold
but my life has been told.

As I drifted off to sleep,
my tears froze.
I could only weep,
I vaguely remember seeing you,
through my frozen eyes,
with slush in my mouth
made of blood and tears,
I've kept in for too many years,
from the night, I lost you.

You ran to me,
you even called my name.
I heard you,
but I couldn't tell you.
I saw you,
but I couldn't hold you.
I loved you,
but I couldn't kiss you.

I longed for you that night,
as I put up my hardest fight,
In the end, I passed on into the light,
hoping to see your eyes one last time,
as you held me in your arms ever so tight.

I know I did though,
see you that last time,
as your warm tears came and met mine,
touching my frozen face.

You put me in the car,
taking me onward,
but I'd already gone upward.

I know you loved me,
more so than any other, ever.
Please know, I'd have given my life for yours
in any situation whatsoever,
that chance, now, I'll have never.
I've begun my next endeavor,
but I'll always love you forever...

# Stuck On Cloud #8

Penticton, British Columbia – March 2002

Been noticing a lot
of fun's going on
in the cloud
up above me.

Just last week, I got
hit by another falling
bottle of fine wine

and woke up the next day
covered in party favors!

Boy, they sure seem
never to slow down.
I had an invite once,
to come up and join them,
but I second guessed it,
stayed home,
and watched celebrity poker.

Maybe I should have taken that
chance though;
I'm too passive to get in the flow;
and just get up and go!
I get caught up doing what I always do,
never setting foot outside just doin'
the things I always do.

They're always laughing and smiling,
never having worries,
that hold you back,
keep you down,
lay you flat.

The *Boss* told me that
it's like hearing your
favorite joke
for the first time,
over and
over,
and over, again.

Or it's like sleeping
out on a camping trip,
waking up in the
morning light,
it's warm,
hitting your face,

opening your eyes to the
deepest,
cleanest,
mountain breath
your lungs have ever tasted,
and you smile and realize
that this is a moment
you'll want to live
1,000 more times!

I'm thinking
I should take him up
on that invitation.
It's just one beat
I didn't make,
one chance,
I didn't take,
a few more steps down
the road less traveled,
but a lifetime of difference
livin' on cloud # 8...

# Another Amazing Day

*Sunday, November 30, 2003*

Mayan Beachfront, Tulum, Mexico – June 2004

Another amazing day
with you,
I put into memory.
These small moments,
are adding up quickly now.

I think I'll store this one,
next to the one of you
burning my breakfast in bed
last week for my birthday,
and crying,
while I tried to hide my smile;

so sweet.

Or perhaps I'll stick it next to
the one of you taking charge,
and buying me
ice cream on our second
date, but forgetting your
wallet;
so cute.

It's quite impressive
how you drift through
my mind now,
like you've been there all
along.

Filling up my past memories
with smiles and happiness
and
penciling yourself into
all of my future thoughts
and dreams...

# Starting Over

*Saturday, November 22, 2003*

Slanted Sunrise Over The Serengeti, Tanzania – January 2004

The newspaper hit the door
at six sharp.
The birds talked amongst themselves,
about how their nights were.
The sun pried my shades apart,
and crawled from my ear to my eyelids
and sizzled them with heat.
Wake up!

I ignored the sun,
I rolled over,
towards her pillow.
Empty.
Gone.
Lost.
This woke me up,
much to the sun's dismay.

Thinking to last night,
driving home,
arguing;
honestly, I don't remember
what for,
or why
it was so important,
that I had to be so right.

I made her cry, and
ruined her make-up,
on our anniversary.
We never got to dinner,
at our favorite restaurant,
and more importantly,
back home.

She ran out,
and I drove off.
Couldn't swallow my pride,

and where has it gotten me?

Perhaps, to a good place,
where I can step back and see,
how much she means to me.

I can't win every single time,
nor can she.
That's why it's called a
relationship.

I give,
she gives,
we live.

Today I'm starting over.
I'm putting her ahead of me.
I don't need to always be right.
She won't always be wrong;
I hope she'll forgive me though,
'cause I'm dying now that she's gone...

Pine Tree Sunset, Saipan, Northern Marianas – June 2001

## Your Choice

*Tuesday, January 27, 2004*

Close your eyes.

Breathe.

No.
Slower.

Fingers dancing on your stomach,
softly, swiftly, not scratching, but

dancing.

They trek up from your hips,
to your stomach,
back around to your loves, and

keep moving.

Up past your ribcage,

both hands,
tugging your shirt,

                                        upwards.

Off.

Hands are back
to your shoulder blades.

Breaths are deeper now.
My hands come around front,
a bit stronger,

                                        clutching now,

tantalizing,
pestering,
baiting.

Collarbone to neck,
softly, tickling,

                                        warmth;

grasping cheek bones,

                                        coming closer.

Fingers on ears,
pulling,
caressing,

                                        closer.

Hands finding their way to
the back of your head,
fingering your hair.
Teeth nibbling a lobe,
pulling you back,

                                        face to face.

The closer you come
to my lips,

                                        in time,

the nearer,
in time,
you come.

                                        It's your choice...

# Coming Back Home

*Monday, November 17, 2003*

Not by choice,
I'm gonna miss his voice.
The way he rocked me to sleep,
and held me when I'd weep.

Bonzai Cliff, Saipan, Northern Marianas – August 2001

His gentle hand was always there
for me,
pushing me on my first swing,
or pushing me to strive harder in
everything that I'd done.

Putting it into words,

hurts.
I'd rather be laughing and smiling,
about always having you there.
But I'm not going to be able to
anymore.

All I can ask for
is that
I'll make it home
in time,
to hold you in my arms
when you leave,
as you did,
when I arrived...

# If You Wait For Me

*Thursday, November 06, 2003*

Managaha Island, Northern Marianas – July 2001

I'm here for you,
my love.
I always have been,
and always will be;
waiting for you and your
arms to embrace me again.

I know you've traveled far,
and the hands of time are
moving,
faster than we want them to;
trying to find a hole
in our love.

Keep me in your dreams,
as you are in mine,
and our hearts will
lead us back
together anew and
you'll have the love
from your thoughts,
in your arms once more,
if you wait for me...

# Trying To Forget

*Thursday, September 25, 2003*

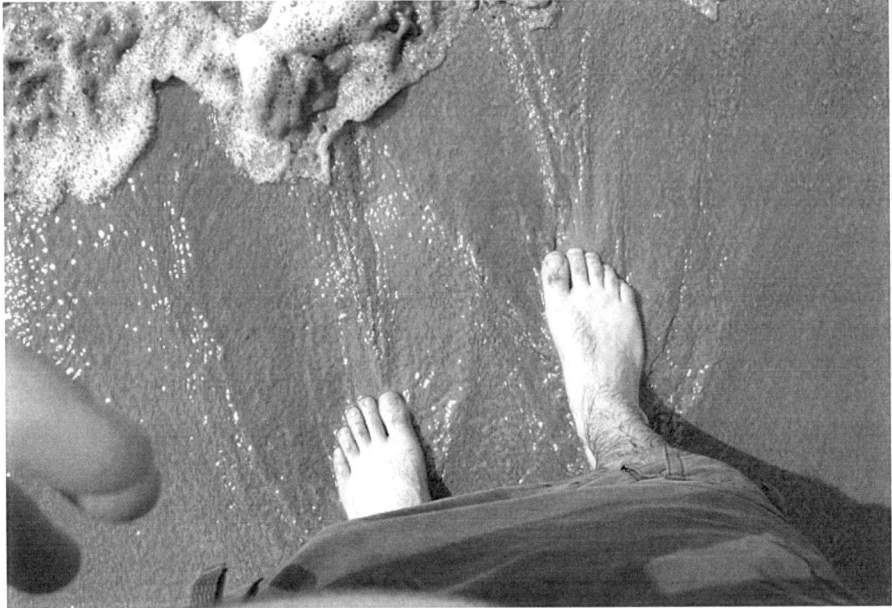

Juhu Beach, Bombay, India – January 2003

The more I try to forget about you,
the more it seems I can't.
But eventually, I'm gonna have to move on,
'cause you won't be there to help me through it all anymore.

I'm gonna go out with other people,
talk and try to have a good time.
Thinking of what you would have worn, or
what you would have said;
Or, when you would have leaned over the table
to kiss me on the forehead
'cause I made that stupid face, you always laugh at.

It won't be you,
and my heart knows the truth,

I try and I try to think about how it would be,
with another you.
I can trick my mind, but my heart knows the truth.

You've torn at my heart time, and time again,
broken it more than I would have preferred,
touched it in so many more ways,
than anyone in my life has ever been able to do.

God how hard it is
to get over the one that made you.
Songs and memories are but a constant reminder.
I can't see myself living a day without you,
you've left footprints on my heart,
and I'm so glad they'll never be erased...

# Her Tears

*Tuesday, October 28, 2003*

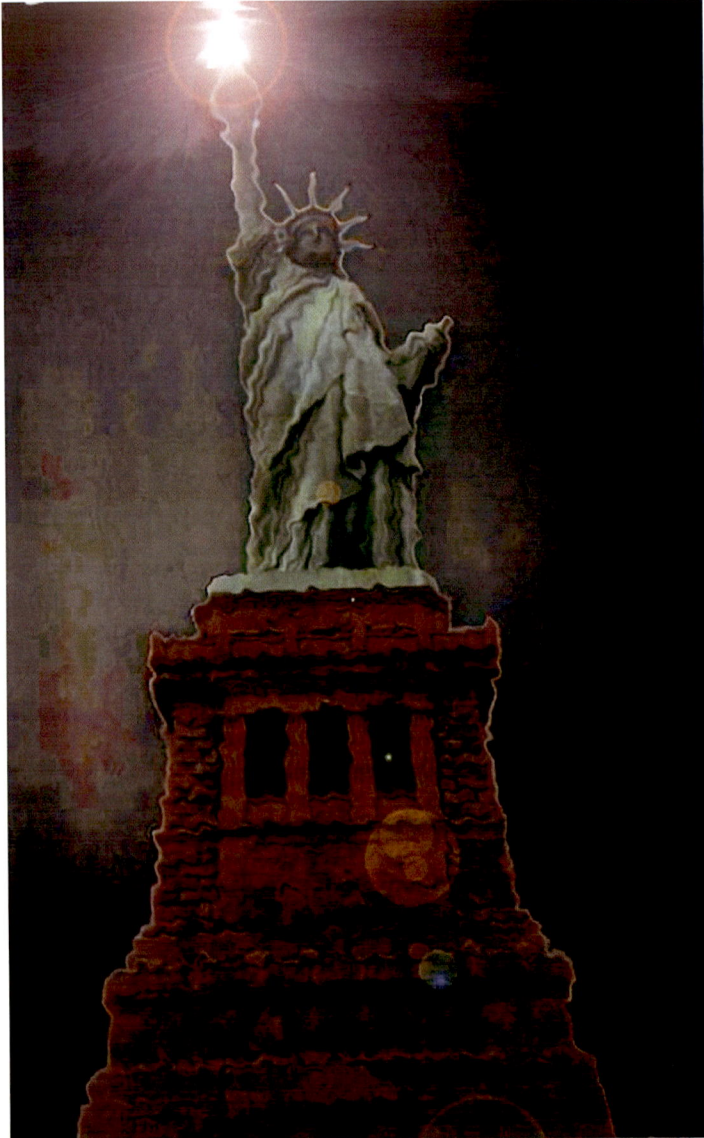

Rippled Liberty, New York City – 2004

The moon lights the lake,
             from the dock,
       clear, cloudless.
Stars sparkle on the water,
             calm, smooth.
       A ripple is made
by a tear,
             from her face,
       that I created;
ruining the
             beauty and perfection,
       of the jet black mirror,
and the love we were meant to have...

# Winning Her Heart

*Wednesday, December 17, 2003*

Ton Sai Bay, Koh Phi Phi, Thailand – June 2002

Winning her heart,
isn't likely to be done by
being passive;
giving in,
resigned,
holding back,
waiting.

Nor is it to be won by
over-pursuit;
aggressiveness,
demanding,
which, inevitably will lead
to suffocation of
the love.

Let the love breathe,
and it will prosper.
A steady mix of both
will work wonders.

Trust me my friend,
the miracles of the heart,
have yet to be mastered,
odds are,
never will;
but the pursuit of the prize,
is at the end of a
very thin line;
traipse it in balance,
and you're well on your way,
to winning her heart...

# When You Come Back To Me

*Tuesday, October 07, 2003*

Bird Island Beachscape, Saipan, Northern Marianas – June 2001

I imagine that I'll be standing there,
grinning, maybe even crying.
Seeing you for the first time
in such a long one.

I will wrap my arms around you,
touching the small of your back,
with my bare hands,
smelling your sweet scent.

I won't know what to say though.
Perhaps, we'll just say nothing,
interwoven in one another's arms,

bethinking.

Remembering back when we had
something more tangible.
Nonetheless, you're my memory now,
only to be visited in my dreams.

But fret not,
we may just have it again someday,
when we see eye to eye,
and you come back to me...

# If I Had It To Do Over

**Monday, October 06, 2003**

Bird Island, Saipan, Northern Marianas – June 2001

I'd not have moved so fast
maybe
I'd have prepared my soul
maybe
I'd have trusted my head
maybe
not put so much trust in my heart.

It's let me go a time or two,
led me in the wrong direction,
or
maybe
it was the right direction,

but the wrong person.

Either way,
it's done it, again.
What I told it not to do.
Fallen.

I'd not have assumed
something would go wrong,
it doesn't always.
Maybe
I'm just unlucky in love.

But like I've done,
time, and time again,
I've learned something.
Haven't I?

I hope that I find out,
what it is I'm learning,
before my heart
tells me it's had enough

trying,
giving,
loving,
leaving...

# Last Night

*Monday, October 06, 2003*

Lake Sunrise, E Unoto, Tanzania, Africa – January 2004

Last night,
    the room was filled with
warmth,
yearning
and trust.

Our bodies entangled in a semblance
    of desire,
hope,
future.

This morning,
    a soft smile,

a kiss as you left.


As I lie there,
   breathless, new like most mornings,
      smiling,
         remembering,
            reminiscing.

I had no idea
   that last night,
      was our last night...

# It's What I Wanted, Right?

*Friday, October 03, 2003*

For you to drift away
from me and my heart.

To give me some space,
so that I could breathe.

I'm not a relationship person, or
maybe I'm scared of having one.

Ngorongoro Crater, Tanzania, Africa – January 2004

For I've had them before,
and obviously,
they didn't work out well then.

So why am I ruining this one?

I believe that I could make it work,
but instead,
I'm holding something back.

I wish that I knew what it was,
because this one is headed south.

You deserve me, times 10,
and I'm only giving you,
one-half of me.

Now that you're leaving,
all I have to show is a
sore heart,
and wet eyes...

But it's what I wanted, right?

# Later

Seattle, Washington – July 2003

We'll have time to get to know
one another.
I know we're moving fast,
but it feels right!

Later

I'll have a chance to tell you
how alluring your laughter is, or
what kind of music I like,
the food that I like to eat,
and the importance of family to me.

Later

We can talk about our issues,
our problems that we're facing.
I like you, but actually,
...oh, it can wait, until

Later

It's all coming to a head now,
we never said anything about
how we felt, what we wanted,
we lived for the moment.
Sounds good at the time,
but it bit us in the ass!

I enjoy your company,
but I can't say how I really feel,
cause we always thought we'd work
it out

Later

Well, it's been "later" now,
for about a week,
no calls, no emails,
no visits.

That day, maybe my head was just
stabbing for ANY words.
Trying to think of a way to
mend what could be the best
thing that ever happened to me
and "later" came out before
I could say,
your laughter is alluring...

# Falling In Love Again

*Thursday, October 02, 2003*

Lake Manyara, Tanzania, Africa – January 2004

Come up from behind me,
in the morning,
at the kitchen sink;
kiss my neck.

Hands on my stomach,
a bit cold,
but so full of passion.
You've fallen in love,

again,

Like every morning
the same...

# Please Don't Stop

*Thursday, October 02, 2003*

Windmills, Walla Walla, Washington – March 2002

We've got a month or two,

under our belts now.

It's nice,

the way things are going.

You treat me well,

and respect my friends.

My family (and I) think

you've hung the moon.
It's amazing,
really.
Please don't stop!

It's nice having someone again,
like you.
I wish you'd stay closer
sometimes, but I understand.
You're a little stand-offish,
from your last broken
heart.

I'll be nice, I promise!
You won't have any regrets!
I'll be twice the person,
no, thrice!
Just for you,
but
please, don't stop.

I think I've gone too
far though,
for what you're giving back!
Uh oh!
I may be in a bit deeper than

what you're showing,

I can't stop now though,

because that's the sort of person I am!

Truly,

madly,

deeply,

adoring,

for you.


I can't help falling, but

you're going the other way!

What more can I do?

I bend this way or that just for you.

Leaving,

drifting,

begging,

crying,

losing.


Please.


        Don't.


                Stop...

McDonald Pass, Helena, Montana – December 2001

# Permanent

*Thursday, September 25, 2003*

We agreed it'd be better to call it off, today.
The time and distance was too much to take.
A tear fell from my eye,
but you never saw,
you never heard,
cause I never let it show.

I played it off as if it was the right decision.
I knew that it was what you wanted, and
I was holding you back.
You were the girl of my dreams,
still, I let you slip through my fingers.
But it won't be permanent,

because I know I can get you back.

If you love something,
let it go, so I did.
I knew in my heart,
that we were made for one another.
I also knew that when the time was right,
we'd be back together.

A year has now passed,
we haven't kept much in touch.
I don't know what you've done;
or, if you care for me much.
But, I thought I'd give you a call,
since I still need you.
Friends? Lovers?
I don't know; but, I need a part of you in me.


Your mom answered the phone
we got caught up on the past.
I've always liked her.
She told me about how you were.
She even told me about how many times
you used her shoulder for me.
Time, and time again, for the rough times,
that we went through.

Some bad things, yes, I've done them,
some bad, you've done some too.
But to this day, I'm still on your mind.
You talk about me to your mom,
nearly every day.
God, how that made me glow inside,
I've wanted to hear that for almost a year now.

I thought of asking for your new number.
Instead, I asked for your address.
I didn't know how or why,

yet, I thought I'd give it a shot.
I asked your mom to keep it a secret,
'cause it was gonna be a surprise.

Thoughts rushed through my head
as I cruised over to your house.
My mind was wandering back and forth.
What would you think?
I knew you'd be happy to see me, right?
I'd run up to you.
I'd hold you in my arms and
swear to never let you go again.

Apparently, God had different plans for me.
Across the yellow line, came the semi into my lane.
As my mind was drifting, thinking of you,
the 18-wheeler crushed my trailer into the rail.

I'm sorry I couldn't have swerved,
it was a corner.
I didn't realize I couldn't open my eyes,
my arms were limp, my breath was short.
Where was I?
A few seconds were all it took to understand.
At least my last thoughts were the best I ever had.

I'm sorry that I didn't tell you earlier,
I wished we had stayed together.
I was so sure that we'd be back together someday.
I guess I'll have to wait a little longer
now to have you forever.
I know I'll get you back, tough
Because even this won't be permanent...

# As I Watched

*Friday, October 17, 2003*

Slanted Waves Rolling In, Cancun, Mexico – June 2004

I watched the waves
roll up on the shore,
in the same pattern,
the same rhythmic beat,
minute after minute,
hour after hour.

It brought me back from
the hidden beaches I lied on,
to your house,
and into your room,
to lie my head upon your chest.

I remembered each, and every, night,
I'd fall asleep there,
and could honestly feel our hearts
thumping,
together.

The same rhythmic beat,
minute after minute,
hour after hour,
For what I hoped would be
forever.

Take care, my dear,
in whatsoever your mind wants
and desires.
But remember, as you're out
searching,
you will always have
a heart
that beats with yours,
inside me...

# Her Scent

*Wednesday, October 15, 2003*

As I lie here,
I see her next to me,
In my mind
because my heart knows,
she's gone.
      Her legs,
      her back,
      her smile,
      her scent
I miss it.

I miss it like the rain
      misses the grass
      in the cold winter.

I miss it like the touch
      of a mother
      long since passed away.

I miss it more than
      color in my paintings,
      like images in
      my mind.

I miss her unequivocally.

For
      at this moment,
      I would give every
      breath I've taken,
      every word I've spoken,

every dream I've dreamt.

For one soft kiss from
      her mouth;
      one precious touch of
      her small hand.

Cause right now,
      I'm living on
      one last relish,

of her scent...

Xel Ha, Mexico – May 2004

# My Angel

*Friday, October 10, 2003*

Heather and Wiley, Bend, Oregon – March 2004

If the sun didn't come out,
the clouds didn't fill the sky,
and the rain kissed the ground,
all day, every hour,
it'd still be one of the best days
of my life.

For today, I woke up next to an angel.

An angel
without wings,
or a halo,
or a long white blouse.

My angel had on,

my T-shirt,
one sock,
and half a scrunchy in her hair.

Her eyes opened today,
to see me smiling,
watching her sleep.

I kissed her forehead,
right between her gorgeous eyes,
and she went back to sleep,
peacefully.

For she knew that I loved her,
and I always will.
She then wrapped her arms,
around my neck and squeezed.
Tight enough to say,
thank you,
for being you,
and loving me...

# No Need To Reminisce

Tulum, Mexico – June 2004

I'm gonna live today
and forget about yester.
She let too much build up,
and just let it fester.
Ideas and thoughts seem to find
a way of twisting in the mind;
it appears to me, that
love may not be so blind!

Perhaps, maybe just
a little near-sighted,
no point though,

I didn't wanna fight it.

Just let 'er go.
Just let 'er rip.
Take the whole glass,
Not just a little sip.

Tongue lashing,
ego bashing,
teeth gnashing,
bad memories we just
keep rehashing!

We've gotten here,
'cause we didn't fear,
what happened before.
We've lived today,
everyday,
and built a bond
on trust and respect
that won't
and can't
be broken by what happened
before you and me were
you and me!

I hope that you can deal.
You know how I feel
about you now,
and that should be enough
to show that our love's tough.
We can make it through this;
love's remiss,
one soft kiss,
no need to reminisce...

# Burn The Town

**Friday, February 13, 2004**

Walla Walla, Washington – March 2002

It's where you were born,
where you grew up.
They are places that you smiled in, and
the air that filled your
young lungs.

It's where you met your best
friend,
and your worst enemy.
It's where you watched your
brother split,
finding love and success outside,
hoping to follow soon.

It's where you watched your sister
fall in love,
and fall to her knees when he left,
but surge on because of your plight.

It's where you saw your family,
falling apart,
for the worst reasons,
and shed tears that still
occasionally fall.

This is the place that you made
friends with so many,
and lost touch with nearly all,
but the ones that you've kept,
will be a friend 'till the day
you die,
crying for you
when you leave,
and that's a friendship
that you should cherish
in the deepest sense.

This is the place that you fell
in love,
with the girl that was destined
for bigger and better things,
but she stayed with you,
through a lot of
thick and thin,
'cause you made her mind believe,
and her heart weep.
But you weren't meant to keep that
love,
as you both moved on,
and you both blossomed,

creating and developing
how you both thought you would
in the back of your minds.

There are so many recollections
I'm sure you have about this town.
So many sights and sounds
that'll always stir up a memory,
but you've had your fill of it.
Bust out!

But in doing so,
remember the people that gave you
this chance to see the world,
change a handful of lives,
and to love again!

Some still live in the same house,
have the same life,
and the same view,
that they've always enjoyed.
They may have not had the
curiosity,
the desire,
the hope, and
the dreams,
that come in some of us.

Big dreams
in a small town
won't work.
Sometimes, big dreams in a big town
don't work.
Find the balance,
think big,
live tomorrow, today,
live today,

thinking that tomorrow
might make yesterday
a little nervous!

Warn the friends and family though,
that
aside from a few strong
bridges
you've helped build,
you're gonna get out,
and burn the town...

# Growing Up (Choices)

Tinian, Northern Marianas – June 2001

Always living life on a whim,
has its obvious ups and downs.
You've always got the upper hand,
Not worrying about the result;
changing your mind,
changing your fate.

It's a nice break from the status quo;
To go out on your own,
to choose your own path.

Life is an adventure;
you never know what's truly out there,
unless you find it for yourself!

Who knows how much of your life should
be spent searching for things that are unclear;
my family tell me one thing,
my friends say another.
But neither tells a truer story than
what I've decided for myself!

I will decide my avenue,
I have chosen my destiny,
thus far.
Still, there have been people in my life,
who seem to make me
want to try
a new route,
to enjoy a new face, or
to kiss another lip.

The choice then becomes to decide
whether
it's worth staying for,
or worth leaving for
because,
I may hide my heart well,
with walls around,
that are guarded heavily;
but something tells me that this might
be a good place to rest my legs
before I take my next plight...

# You Won

*Monday, March 19, 2004*

Saipan Storm, Northern Marianas — August 2001

You might not understand,
but hey,
I don't expect you to.

Time went by,
your thoughts didn't include me.
My thoughts, of you,
never really left.

Soon enough, it was time to move on,
My heart had suffered enough,
and needed another to love,
I thought you'd do the same,

which drove me even harder
to find a way to fill this pain.

The plans we had made together,
we let slip through our
young fingers,
and while there were
others that thought
I was for them,
they lost,
and you won.

You did.
After you moved away;
after you had found
the arms of someone else,
to hold you like
I never would again.
You chose another life path,
and we quit talking.
I pretended as if you'd
quit breathing,
quit holding,
quit caring,
and I ignored you,
when you needed me most.
That sorrow will never fade.

Many years have gone by,
and I knew it was over,
but now,
we have a chance again.

You're where you are,
and I'm where I've always been.
Keeping the door open
in my heart;
a door to which only
one has the key,

only one has ever held the key,
I lost,
but you won.

I remember all of our best times,
were when our hearts beat as one.
The time is on us now,
and the decisions we made
so long ago
are going to come
full circle,
when we both realize
that I've lost,
and you've won...

# Little Things

*Tuesday, February 10, 2004*

Lyin' inside everyone,
waitin' and probably
needin' to explode,
                        BOOM!
Bustin' out your worst,
not knowin' or carin'
the result of the
words that you're spinning,
droppin' dirty f-bombs,
like you've never been.

Sometimes it just needs
to happen though!

Andy Tillo Thesis Piece, Walla Walla, Washington – April 2001

It's beggin' to get out,
needs some feeds,
as it breathes,
asking for a chance to
show what's hidin',
kept from shinin'.
You've gotta let him out though,
or somethin' worse might
happen.

He's angry and wants to rage
at somethin',
anythin'.
Can't talk to him,
won't talk to her,
just gonna let it sit,
and wait,
till somethin' pushes
too hard, and again
it'll bubble up,
askin' to be set free,
wantin' to see
goin' on a blasphemy spree,
one,
two,
                    THREE!

Hell, this ain't me!
I don't agree!

Oh, it's you,
I guarantee!

Keep it in and breathe.
Don't let him leave,
tryin' to deceive,
wipe it on your sleeve!

Ignore it,
trash it,
dump it,
not worth it...

# It Might Be Love

*Monday, February 09, 2004*

Budding Beach, Cancun, Mexico – June 2004

If she's in your dreams,
before you wake

In your arms,
as you wake

And in your heart,
when you're awake...

Demons Within, Saipan, Northern Marianas – June 2001

## Everyone Has Ghosts

*Thursday, February 05, 2004*

In the closet,
hanging out with the
skeletons, there's ghosts
lying in wait to be
exposed.

You decide whether
they'll be
shown to everyone,
or kept in the back
and taken to the grave.

It's a choice everyone
has had to make
or someday
will have to
make in a lifetime.

Keep them hidden for
too long, and it may
seem like they've never
really happened.

But remember,
they're called ghosts
and skeletons for a reason...

# The Blue Shoe Mystery

Stop #5, The Blue
Par 2, Handicap 12

Walsh looking as happy as always,
Tillo looking normal...

"I think I'm done, take me home"
--Eric after nut shot
"If you ever go to a bar, don't order a nut shot, it sucks"--Eric
"Do you think Dr. J could beat Toivola and a Stegasaurus one-on-one?--Joe
"We can make fun of him when he is barfing"--Joe about TBT

Walla Walla, Washington – May 2001

Lost one shoe,
because of the brew!

Adieu, adieu,
my stupid shoe.

What'd I do,
with that damn blue shoe?

{Screen goes blurry, that's the cue!}

I last recall,
   that bar's bathroom stall.

For a good time,
  give me a call.

Sounded good at the time!
  A prank call on that line,
all I did was drop one thin dime,
  458-6289!

Write it down,
  put it in your pocket!
Oh hell, the bathroom stall,
  I forgot to lock it!

Excuse me!
I'm in here!
  I thought,
is this not abundantly clear?
  He had no care,
wasn't gonna chuck just air!
  He was gonna puke,
right then, and there,
  on my porcelain chair!

Uh oh!
Gotta get out!
  Bout that time!
Ain't no doubt!
  This guy's gonna spout!

Ugh. Too late.
  Smells like fish bait.
I reckon that ruined this date.
  Ain't that just great?

Well now, my pants stink,
  can't see getting another drink,
I'll try to wash off in the sink!
  Atta boy! Way to think!

Off with the slacks,
  brush off his puke snacks!
Ok, just gotta relax.
Shoes come off,
  pants come off,
Sounds like he's done in the toilet trough!
  Scoff, scoff!
Cough, cough.
  Hope he liked his stroganoff!

So standing there,
  in my underwear,
warning onlookers to beware.
  Barfy-boy grabs my shoe,
heaving another load of nasty goo!
  Yup, in my shoe.
Indeed. Eww.

  "Friend, please keep my shoe.
With your addition of spew,
  why on earth would I need two?!?!"

The mystery is solved,
  strangely evolved.
How a date dissolved,
'cause Barfy-boy got involved!

# There Is A Place

Lion Rock, Serengeti Plains, Tanzania, Africa – January 2004

*There is a place,*

> in my mind,
> near the back,
> where I find myself
> reliving smiles,
> kisses and memories;
> from a love
> gone right
> at a time, gone wrong.

*Moving on in life,*

> takes you to new places,
> showing you new faces,
> 'round the bases,
> finding new spaces;
> love embraces,
> those who let it
> surround them
> and encases
> a heart with yours
> when time and places
> match the love
> put forth by
> another's traces.

*I loved you, so deeply,*

> I always will,
> but the mind finds space
> where it'll erase
> times gone by
> and will replace
> the memories of your face,
> but in my heart,
> I'll always know,
> there is a place...

# If I Were You

*Thursday, January 22, 2004*

Serengeti Plains, Tanzania, Africa – January 2004

If I were you,
I'd take that step
down the twisted trail,
you've yet to trod.
You've nothing to lose
for it;

perhaps, your inhibitions,
your negative ideas,
and, possibly
your soft heart.
What are you saving it for
in the first place?
You're not going to be able
to save it,
or, store it on a shelf.
It's meant to be shared,
and used by another.
Keeping it locked up
isn't going to make you smile
any larger,
or, laugh any louder.
Perhaps, it'll make you feel
safe, and secure.
But, letting it decide
for itself,
is a feeling
ten-fold any previous emotion!
So, if I were you,
I'd reconsider what you're about to do.
Walls aren't making it any easier,
and your heart isn't getting
any younger.

Believe in what it has to say,

for in the end,

it'll be a love worth dying for

if both hearts

see eye to eye...

# I Have Lost You

*Friday, September 26, 2003*

Serengeti Sunrise, Tanzania, Africa – January 2004

In as many words as I can breathe,

Have not a care for their meaning of truth for you.
And in every step that I've taken since,
Voracious appetite for the love that I once had?
Every person deserves to have that feeling,

Lust and desire for but one.
Out of every vein, I bleed for you,
Stay with me just one more night.
Touch my neck with

Your lips.
Once more,
Unendingly...

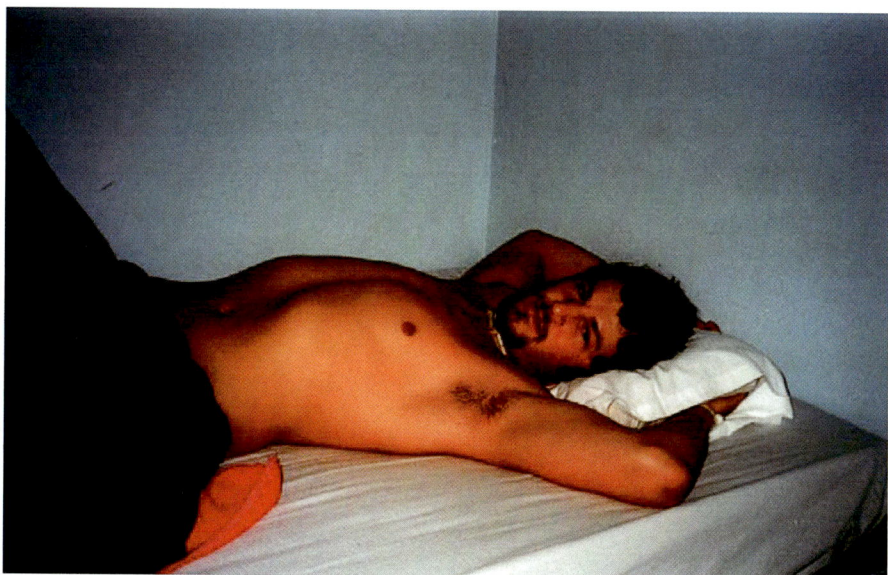

Early To Rise, Koh Phi Phi, Thailand – June 2002

# Make The Night Last Longer

*Monday, October 27, 2003*

Put a blanket over the window,
  to keep the sun from
telling us to stop holding
   one another, and to face the day.

Hit the snooze to give us,
  just nine minutes more
of living in the lap of love
   so deep that the sun will
HAVE to leave us alone.

It won't be able to find us,
  as our eyes close again,
not for sleep,
   but for the passion
we're creating
    by the love we're making...

# That Same Path

*Thursday, October 23, 2003*

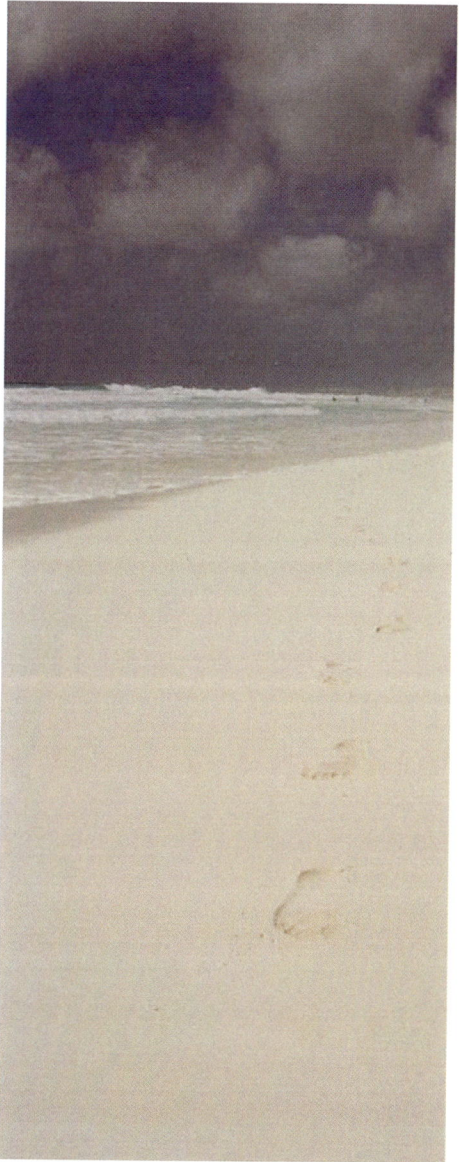

Footprints, Cancun, Mexico – June 2004

Your fingers walk it.
  From my arm pit,
                          down, along my side

    crawling, slowly,
      tickling.


  You're almost asleep,
                              so am I.

    The voyagers take a
  nap here and there, but
                              continue

      to my hip,
  slide over to my stomach
                        to dance for a spell;
          circles.


    Up, back, zig-zag,
  traversing past my breasts,
                            to my neck,
                palming my cheek bone,
        caressing my ear.


  This is the point where I'll
    either get me a good
                            night kiss or,

        as I hope,
  you'll take another lap...

# Always Been There For Me

*Tuesday, October 21, 2003*

You may not know it, but
you've been my dearest friend
since we first met.

Softest heart, kindest soul,
I've known in a while.
So naive,
simple,
beautiful,
pure.

Very unlike the usual crew;
That I always knew.
Who knew I'd be led to you?

I'm not sure how, or why,
but just know, that I'm glad
I met you.

You've made me smile
when there was nothing happy.
Think twice,
when I thought once was enough, and
believed in me, when there
was nothing to believe in.

It could be me against the world,
and you'd be on my side;
giggling and smiling,
and have NO idea why.

But that's quite endearing,
as my friend, and always will be.
I'm sure we have many more years to come,
but at this one, I just hope you realize,
you've shaped my life for the better,
and I'll always be there for you, like
you've always been there for me...

Bonzai Cliff, Saipan, Northern Marianas – June 2001

# Raining On Smilesville

Xel Ha, Mexico – June 2004

We're not doing this for money!
We're not big superstars!
Hell, half of us think our work is funny, honey!
Last night, I was in a bar, with a fat cigar,
listening to some old guy sing on an out of tune guitar.

But, he's smiling, he's not aiming to please, I hope.
He's not out there for eyes that grope.
Self-adulation? Nope!
Most people in here know that he's the local tope,
but God knows, he's trying this slippery slope!

99.9% of us won't be super "poet" famous,
But who could really truly blame us,
for wanting to hear something nice about us.
But you're makin' it rain in Smilesville, you ignoramus!

I know, I'm all for the right to free speech,
but partner, you're kinda like a medicinal leech!
Sucking away lifeblood, bud,
criticizing everyone for not being a stud!

Hell, I have no idea how I write it, I just do.
Yea, I like hearing good things about it too,
I guess that I really never knew,
the smile I'd bring to another person, maybe two.
Hopefully, I'll be able to hook you up too!

For there's a lot of people out there,
that have taken a hit,
for work they've knit,
done up to submit,
and I'll be the first to admit,
that some of them aren't gold
but people on here are bold,
able to mold,
words and phrases their minds unfold,
to be told,
knowing they're not being polled,
odds are, they're not being sold,
and yea, maybe some people are looking to be consoled,
but who cares?

It's human nature to be wanted,
if you've got it, flaunt it!
Everyone that has posted is undaunted,
in their hope not to be taunted,
So yes, when it comes to flattery,
hell yea, I want it...

# To Be With You This Winter

*Monday, October 20, 2003*

Lookout Pass, Montana – December 2002

Underneath the blankets,
our bodies lay ensnarled,
all night long, beneath the flakes
falling down
to the cabin rooftop.

The fire is dying down,
in the furnace,
but lighting up,
in our hearts.

The smell of the marshmellows,
chocolate burning,

logs, and tree brush
in the open fire.

The sound of the river,
rippling by,
crashing over the rocks
in search of it's home,
at the lake.

The touch of your lips,
upon my skin.
Salty, with our bodies,
sliding on each other,
pulsating,
grinding,
meshing,
living,
climaxing.

It's my favorite season
for love, you know...

# Love's Countin' On It

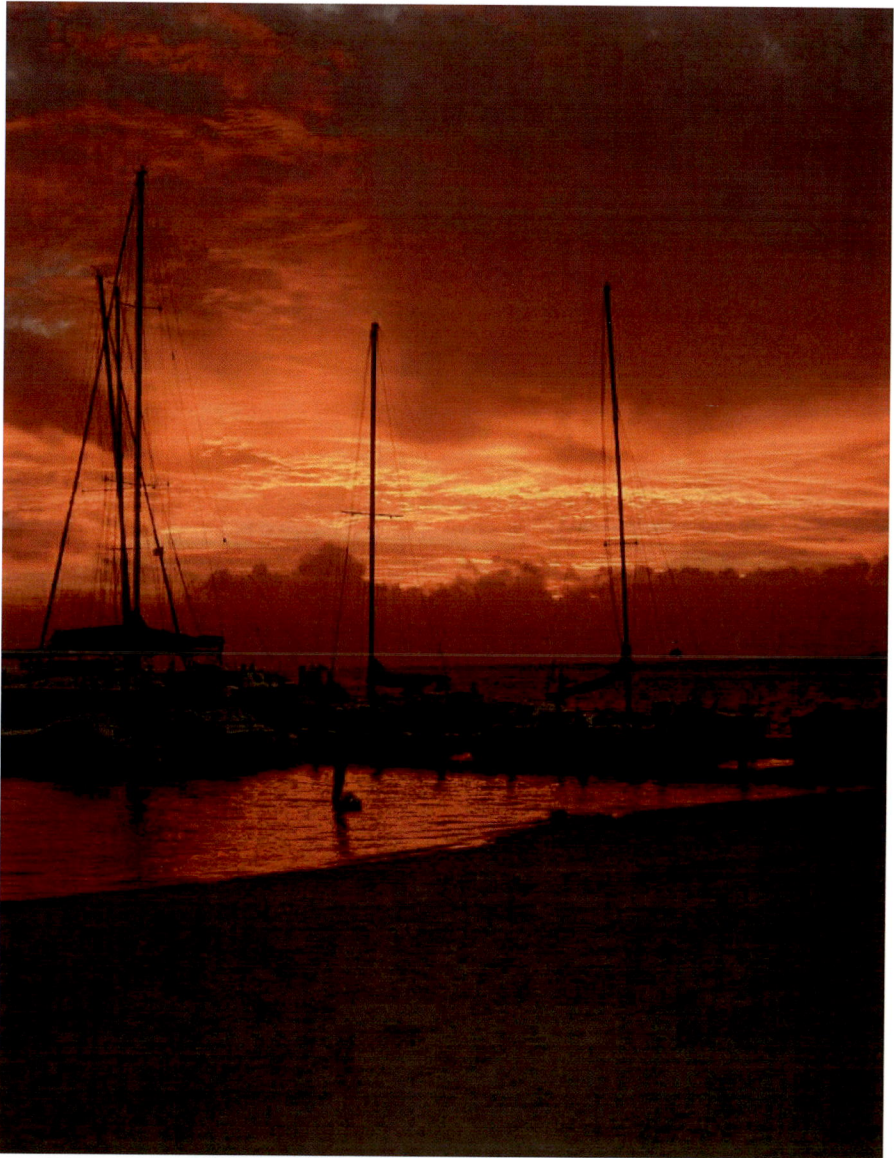

Ships Sunrise, Cancun, Mexico – June 2004

Sometimes, she's not sure,
what she wants out of this,
she's a bit hesitant,
a bit reluctant,
to have it crumble,
like so many times before.

The past has been
anything
but mindful
of her feelings.
She's tentative
to give it her all.

She's learning
that I'm not always so
serious.
I'm laid back; yet
still intrigued by her.

I suppose that
I express it differently
than her past choices.
A new look for her,
but she's learning, I think.

It's a new step in her life,
as it is for me.
Putting my heart on the line
hasn't come for quite some time.

Putting your trust in someone
doesn't happen overnight,
but develops over time.
Feelings grow,
people learn,
love evolves.

I think she's getting
a grasp for me,
learning how I am,
what I do,
and I'm learning how she
is, and what she does,
that's why it's called
a relationship.

However, from time to time,
I think that I need to realize,
her feelings are on the line
as well,
and needs to be reassured
that I'm going to be there for her.

I'm workin' on it,
she's thinkin' on it,
we're buildin' on it,
'cause
love's countin' on it...

# She Told Me

*Friday, January 02, 2004*

She told me something that
I didn't know about her,
this morning,
while we tussled in bed.

Not the nicest,
nor prettiest thing that
I've heard from her lips.
Perhaps,
the words even stung a bit;
near piercing.

I didn't know how to react,
so, I played it off
as if I didn't hear her.
I shrugged,
kissed her neck softly.

It had nothing to do with me,
something from the past.
It wasn't her choice,
against her will, even.

I'm angered for the moment;
rage and hate can build;
maybe she just
wanted to tell me when
we were smiling, while
in each others arms.

But that's why it's called
the past,
I guess.

She's with me for a reason, and
perhaps, she wants me to know
all about her.

As much as it may burn now,
my ears,
her mouth,

Fleeing Zebras, Serengeti Plains, Tanzania, Africa – January 2004

our hearts;
the future won't change
because of the past
at the present...

# Take Me (At Her Bedside)

*Monday, November 03, 2003*

Metropolitan Museum of Art, New York City, New York – February 2002

Take me,
in hand,
as we were when we were younger;
care free.
Along the trail, we walked so many
times;
lost in one another's eyes,
creating,
believing,
showing,
craving
one another until the day had stopped,
and we found ourselves

lost again,
but in each others dreams.

with you,
back to when we hadn't worried
about what we didn't have,
but how we were blessed,
with what we did;
away from the arguments,
the fighting,
the bickering,
the crying,
the lying,
the hiding, and the
leaving.

back to last summer,
after too many years;
longing,
missing,
searching,
hoping.

We found each other,
renewed;
so much easier to talk
through the small problems,
now;
thanks for finally listening,
and understanding.
It's nice to be forever
yours again,
finally.

instead,
as she's done nothing,
but give me what I've always
dreamt,
cared for me as if I was the only

one on earth,
and believed in me,
as I believe in You;
but if someone must go,
please take me away,
and let MY angel
breathe another day...

# Did You Know That I Watched You?

*Friday, September 26, 2003*

Through Other Eyes, Saipan, Northern Marianas – July 2002

From the corner of my eye, all of the time,
I'd be talking to a person, but you were behind.
My eyes would sometimes critique you,
on what you'd say, or who you'd be with too!

Until the day that I met you with that friend.
Your eyes so deep blue,
I could see into you.
I know that you noticed me.
We talked long into the night.

~~~~~~~~~~~~~~~~~~~~~~

Yes, I knew that you did.
I remember the times when you'd be looking for me.
I wanted you to find me,
I wanted you to take me new places.
I had envisioned many things with you,
I clearly wanted the man that I couldn't have.

I couldn't be the woman I wanted to be,
I wanted you for your mind.
Your mind gave off vibes I'm sure that your heart mimicked.
Oh, to be yours for a night or two, or an eternity...

# The Man I Am

*Friday, September 26, 2003*

Andy Tillo Thesis Artwork, Walla Walla, Washington – May 2001

I don't think of where it was,
I think of when.
I haven't thought of, after you,
'cause you're still here.

The color I put into my artwork,
didn't come from a brush.

It was in your touch,
your smell.

I don't know why this fantastic heart
blessed me.
I wish that it was still here sometimes though,
to catch mine,
as it may fall again,
onto a harder
ground...

# I Forgot About You

*Tuesday, September 25, 2003*

Rattlesnake Ridge, Washington – February 2004

I forgot about you today,
I forgot about your gentle smile,
your warm touch,
your sweet smell.
I forgot about your soft hair,
your smooth skin,
and your flawless eyes.
I forgot about how you make me feel right,
when everything else feels wrong.
I forgot about how you make 4 days
seem as if they were 30 seconds.
I forgot about how I can't help falling for you.
I forgot about how perfection has touched my hands.

I forgot about how thinking of you often brings tears to my eyes.
I forgot that you'd never break my heart.

Today I forgot about the sunflowers in your eyes.
I forgot about how you laugh at all my stupid jokes.
I forgot about how you think that I hung the moon.
I forgot about how you changed my idea of perfect.
I forgot about how nobody has been a better friend.
I forgot about how you mean the world to me.
I forgot that you'll be mine someday.
Today wasn't any different from any other day though,
Cause I forget about you 1,000 times, everyday...

# You Stole My Heart

*Wednesday, October 29, 2003*

Hidden Ship, Saipan, Northern Marianas – June 2001

It had been hidden;
behind walls,
locked doors,
for so long.

Stepped on, smashed,
dumped
and broken too often to
keep tabs.

It hurt too much,
every time
love was on the line,

to let someone touch,
what I needed to be mine.

I let my guard down,
you broke the walls down,
knocked the doors down,
and picked my heart up off
THE ground!

I didn't mean to let you inside,
but now that you're here,
maybe you could stay a while.

All I ask you of my heart,
to take good care-
you're the newfound heir-
of a love I swear
will be there.

You stole my heart
from a place I never
wanted it to see;
but you've rescued it,
and put it in the place,
it was always meant to be...

# In Your Hands

Canyonscape, Okanogan, Washington – March 2002

In your hands right now,
you hold my face,
caressing,
kissing,
touching.

                              I believe it's something special,
                                the way that your hands can
                              maneuver their way around my
                                                        body,

as if they've always been,
meant to dance on my
skin.

All I ask is a chance,
love,
support,
structure,
in a relationship because
I can't be hurt again.

The last time
hurt me far too deeply.

Please take care of your hands,
for they carry precious cargo.
Hopes,
dreams,
thoughts,
passion,
lust,
desires,
love.

Above all else, I ask you,
I'm pleading,
please be cautious,
because
right now,
my soft heart lies,
in your hands..

# You Make Me Smile Inside

*Wednesday, October 01, 2003*

Rocks over Serengeti, Tanzania, Africa – January 2004

You make me smile inside,
and nobody has for a long time.
It's not something you've done.
It's something you haven't.

I can usually pick something out,
within a week or two.
Whether it's the way you smell,
or the way you act.

Perhaps, it's the way you kiss,
the way you smile,
the way you walk,
or how you chew your food.

Nope, none of those.

You're not so needy.
You're a strong woman!
You're not too prissy.
You're not mad.

Your touch is heavenly.
Your kiss is gentle.
Your eyes are true.
Your heart is soft.

I can usually pick something out,
that will inevitably lead to,
the demise of the relationship,
but not with you.

I'm not sure if it's a good thing.
I don't know if I'm ready for it.
But all signs point to
giving it a whirl because,
you make me smile inside...

# To My Mother

*Monday, September 29, 2003*

Deer Kisses, Lincoln, Montana – July 1998

Mom, I don't know where to start,
with all you've given me.
> You gave me nourishment when I was young,
> you taught me to crawl, to walk, and to talk.

You taught me that it's not ok to fight with my siblings.
You showed me how to tie my shoes,
> how to make a peanut butter and jelly sandwich,
> and how to write in cursive.

For all these things, I am very grateful.
But more than any other,
> I am thankful you taught me how to use
> my heart.

Yours has been so strong throughout the years,
staying so sincere,

                                    letting loose so many tears,
                            but you were able to persevere.


I can't count the number of times
I've cried with you,

                                        laughed with you,
                                        loved with you.


                    My heart.


It's been put to the test repeatedly.
It's been floating on a cloud,

                                it's been broken to pieces,
                            but none because of you.


You always picked the pieces back up,
put them together again,

                        kissed my cheek,
                    and told me everything would be all right
                        with time.


It did,
and has.

                            For every aspect of my life,
                        I look at what got me where I am.


Sure, my head has helped me here and there,
my hands a time, or two,

                                but most of all, what got me here,
                            was my heart, because of you...

# I'm Struggling

Saipan, Northern Marianas – June 2002

I'm struggling to get by
doing what I'm doing,
with my life, and
with my love.

Every time I decide something,
I get blind-sided by
things I haven't seen;
bringing about a new choice,
a new opportunity.

Whether or not I cease this
occasion, depends upon the
last turn that I made,
while I was
at the last stop sign.

I turned right.

But in retrospect,
a lefty would have put me
in an open valley,
with no roads.
I'd have a bright sky,
and a brighter future.

I'm thinking of swinging
a 180;
hoping it'll bring me,
back to
the things which I've missed
on this winding road,
inevitably leading me back to
the open sky
I've been searching for in
this concrete forest...

# Learning to Love Again

Sunset at Seaside, Saipan, Northern Marianas – September 2001

It's been a few years now,
since we've parted ways.

We had something
I thought
that could last through
time and more so,
through distance.

It didn't.

I remember exactly,
where, when, what, how.
I had a feeling about why,
you left me high and dry.

The phone call that night,
asking me if I recalled the pact,
the one that we made
when I moved away;
or, how we'd say
either way,
if someone else, pulled you astray
was enough to betray
our trust.

I understood.
It's taken a while though;
believe you me!
But now, I find myself in the same
position.

Budding love,
scared,
curious,
nervous,
hoping it wouldn't happen again.
Leaving me;
after giving everything
I had to give.

I think to myself,
It's a new
relationship,
with a new person,
this one has a new chance,
still,
she could drop me just as hard.

Then a voice inside says,
It is true,
you may get hurt
twice as hard as before.

Except,
remember this,
you may also reach heights
that you've never dreamed of
before,

by taking this chance and
learning to love again...

# Gonna Be Cold Outside Tonight

*(At Least She Could Have Let Me Have The Couch!)*

*Friday, December 19, 2003*

Now, I'm not sure if it'll matter, as
I wasn't in a mood to give the woman flatter!
The eggnog was flowing, mixed with the batter!
But, my mother-in-law loves to chatter.
I MIGHT have slipped up and said she may look a little fatter!

Soon, I found out that I'm nearly worthless!
on top of not knowing even how to dress,
or, how my hairline is beginning to regress.
My T-shirt with its beer and bbq, oh
dear God, yes.
it's certainly a mess!

How I won her daughter's heart?
She'll never guess,
'Cause she knew that
I'd never be a success!

Bad idea lady, I'm drunk,
as a skunk!
I understand,
You don't think I'm a hunk!

Glass 2015, Lions Napping, Serengeti Plains, Africa – January 2004

Understandable,
'cause I'm giving off a bit of a funk.

Honestly, have you seen that extra junk
in your trunk?
Uh oh, it's
off to the couch for me!
Sorry dear, that'll happen.

But, since I'm going there anyway,
I might as well get in one last gasp!

Honey, I love every quality
that you've gotten from her.
Her manners are first-class,
yet, at times, maybe a bit crass,
an attitude that has a bit of sass.
But I think that most of all,
I thank God everyday that
you didn't get her ass!

# Never Around, But Always By My Side

*Friday, March 05, 2004*

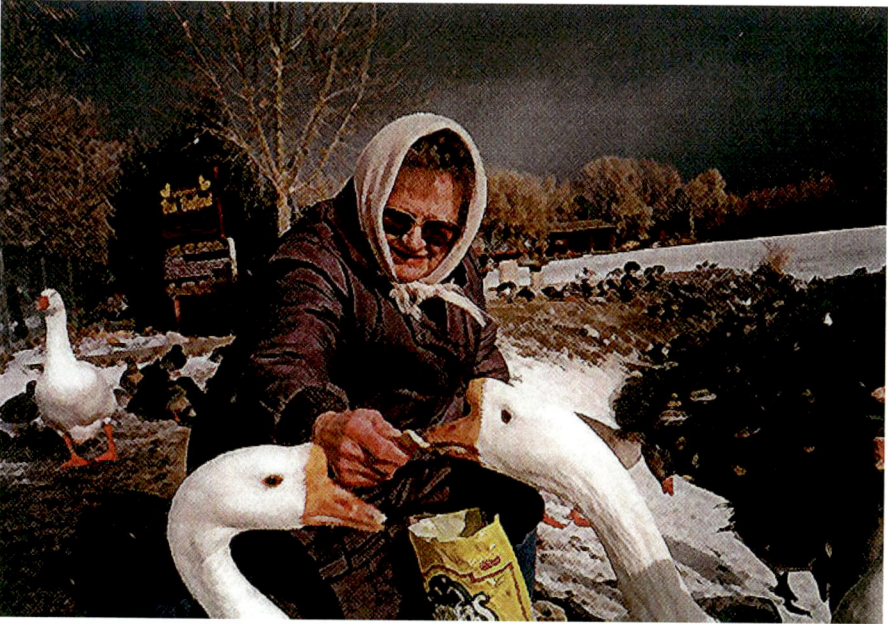

Gramma's Geese, Helena, Montana – 2003

As long as I can remember,
you've been there for me.
In whatever I've done,
wherever I've been,
you've been by my side,
in every decision
I've made.

Occasionally, the time apart
would be longer than
we'd both hoped for,
and the time together
would be far too short to

tell all the stories
brave all the adventures,
and relive all the memories,
but we'd leave just as happy.

No matter what I've gone through,
how the last few years have passed,
you've been there for me,
in that moment.
Our smiles were permanently fixed
upon our transfixed faces,
and our conversations spoke of
many of the same things
that we always talked about,
the weather is nice, and you'll never guess,
I had to shovel snow this morning though!
I talked to your mother last night.
She seems to be doing well, for her anyway.
The mailman brought a lot of nothing today,
except one handwritten letter,
from you,
a note meant just for me
and it made my heart glow,
to know that you still care
for someone that is
never around but
always by your side...

# We Had A Chance

***Tuesday, November 04, 2003***

I remember awhile back,
when the landscape,
and our hearts,
were so green.

Camel Trek, Mombasa, Kenya, Africa – January 2004

Learning new things,
meeting new people,
and losing the ones that
we gave so much to.

It isn't our fault,
that people can drift away,
so easily,

from our soft hearts;
you'll find people like that
throughout life.

But, you'll also find people like yourself,
kind,
inspirational,
compassionate,
endearing,
caring,
loving,
that will grow,
with your soul.

Things happen the way they do
for a reason.
Hey, I got beat to the punch,
but I've kept that spot open,
in my heart,
if you ever want to come visit...

Oceanfront Property, Diani Beach, Kenya, Africa – January 2004

## I Want To

*Wednesday, March 03, 2004*

I want to stay in bed
this morning
with my eyes shut
alarm off
and you, in my arms.

I want to wake up at noon,
forget work,
sleep in
and make you breakfast
in bed.

Before your beautiful eyes
ever see the sun
your nose will smell the
eggs,
coffee,
and toast.

Afterwards, I'll massage
your back, then
kiss your neck,
and play it by ear.

I want to take you
to lunch out on the pier
where we first met.
I'll have the fish n' chips
and you, the clam chowder.
We'll then lie back in our chairs
and bask in the sun.

I want to get you the ice cream,
which you always told me to get
from the store;
third aisle on the right,
with the extra nuts and chocolate!

At the end of the day,
I want to realize that you're in
my arms to stay,
for good this time, perhaps.
We'll watch a movie and fall
asleep again in each other's arms.

I think more than anything though,
I want to call you up,
and quit dreaming about
what might have been,

and instead, think of what I
should have done.
I want to tell you that I didn't
want you to leave.
As much as I said that I didn't mind,
it wouldn't hurt,
I didn't feel,
the pain you felt
about the way we were.

I want to find that love again.
The love that I gave up for nothing.
My life isn't the same any longer
realizing that you're not here
to make my dreams a reality.

I keep telling myself that
I'll find you again,
and our lives will again mesh,
the way that they did when I first
touched your lips.

I want to believe in us again,
and I want you to believe that
I didn't mean what I said
when I told you I didn't
feel the *same way*.
Because the *same way* is making
my heart fall out of my chest
every time that I think of you,
or I smell something with your
scent remaining on it.

I want to have you find
it in your heart
to realize mine's too soft
to be without you
for one more day,
in my lonely world...

# When I Am Finally Laid To Rest

*Monday, September 29, 2003*

When I am finally laid to rest,
what will I look back on as being
my happiest moment?

I was 5 years old,
finally able to go to school,
like my brother,
I ran there!

I was 12 years old,
when I got my first kiss.
Spin-the-bottle is a dangerous game,
at such an age!

I was 14, my father left,
my mother cried,
my family split,
our lives changed.

I was 15, I could drive a car,
3-speed on the column,
it had no brakes,
but I was on the road!

I was 17, I met a girl,
she stole my heart,
and then hid it,
in a place where even she couldn't remember.

I was 18, I went to college,
to learn about the world.
No rules, no parents, just fun.

Mind, body and soul all had their fair share,
of living and learning!

Tunnel of Roots – Tinian, Northern Marianas – April 2004

I was 21, I worked on a tropical island,
in the South Pacific.
I drank margaritas each night,
and smiled with my new friends.

I was 23, I had no money,
I was on the other side of the world,
with my friends,
and the sun on my face.
Hearing the waves pummel the shore,
from my bungalow.

I'm 25, with everything on
the horizon
and all I've ever wanted
in my heart.
All I need to do is

reach out.

I'll be 75, looking back on my life,
reflecting on all the times when I've had regrets.
That 2 seconds will pass quickly,
as I won't have any.

Life, in it's entirety,
is ONE moment,
on a scale,
much bigger than we know.
so if I have to chose
the happiest moment in my life,
I can say,
without a doubt,
that time is now...

# I Heard A Song Today

*Monday, September 29, 2003*

I heard a song today.
Into my ears,
through my mind,
and it spoke to my heart.

I had heard this song before,
but never the intent.
Two separate memories,
two separate times in my life.
You and this melody.

I know that you've moved away, and
I hope that you're happy there.
I hope that someday this song
will float past you,
and that you will remember,
all of our times together.

I heard a song today...

Jazzfest, New Orleans, Louisiana – May 2003

Shipwrecked, Tinian, Northern Marianas – June 2001

# For Two Weeks

*Friday, September 26, 2003*

For two weeks, you were mine in hand.
The friends of the past all drifting off elsewhere,
you and I were breathing in one aura,
for the touch that had been anticipated.

Unassuming.

For three months, you were mine in heart.
time - too short to have any more.

Tears fell,
scents faded,

memories drifted,
life unfolded.

Don't think that it meant nothing,
because it did.
The tears were real,
your touch was genuine,
but mostly,

the memories are forever...

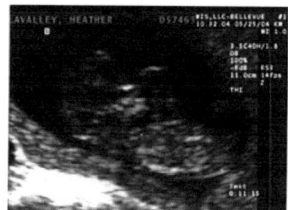

# Shootin' Out The Stars

*Wednesday, February 18, 2004*

With ideas from your head
late at night,
not remembering what you said
the next day.
But, at the time,
the words were so passionate,
thoughts so concrete,
"the next big thing"
was right at our feet.

Goa, India – January 2003

We just need to reach out
and grab it.

Seize the moment,
live the life,
take the chance,
draw the knife
make a stance
move forward to advance
the ideas that you
create
in your brilliant mind
will someday find
paper and solid ground
to build a force.

I wasn't,
and I'm sure the world isn't,
ready to take you on
face-to-face,
as you've got the upper-hand;
you're headin'
off to take
up the time
and make what you make
of the ideas that you create.
It's a challenge
and a plight, which not many
are going to partake in,
but the vision is yours
my friend.

I know you've got
the heart of a lion
in you,
and the eye of a tiger
watching with you,
stepping up

to take on the dreams
that we've had,
and the ideas we've
wanted to live,
but haven't moved
a pawn out to B-4 yet,
the queen hasn't even
gotten her feet wet,
the rook is lookin'
to make the first threat,
but the army is building!

The pieces are almost
in place,
to rock the cage,
front stage,
New York Times front page,
comes of age,
brain has hit full-gauge!

It'll happen soon.
We've both said it,
and both seen it.
The time is drawing nearer,
now,
when the world will be clearer.

Living around you,
breathing in your ideas
and realizin' we'll be as
sure as we've ever been that
the future is ours,
climbin' that big mountain,
we won't worry about the scars
'cause
we'll be
shootin' out the stars...

# One More Guess

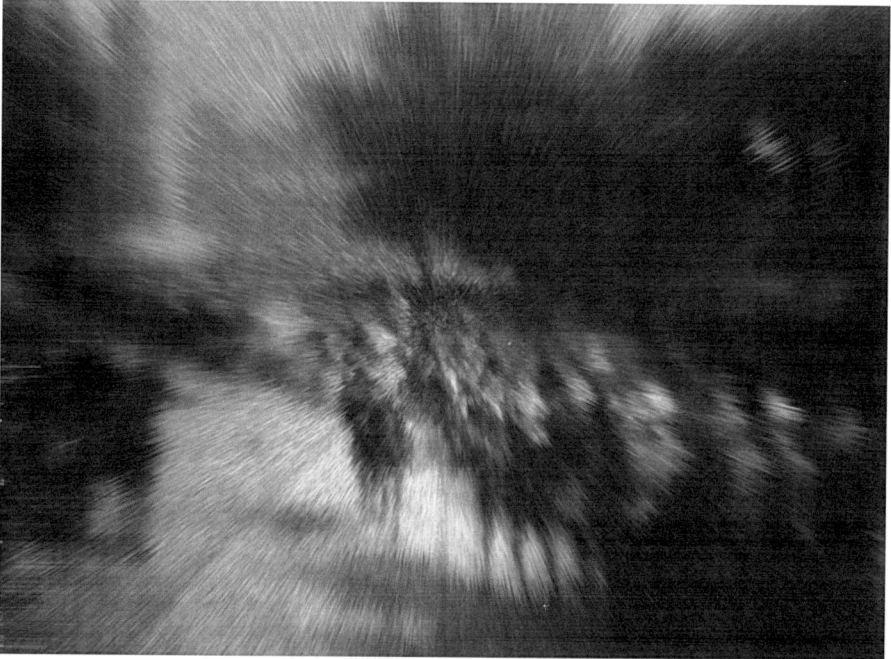

Horserace, Amsterdam, Netherlands – February 2002

At what it was that
drew me into your eyes,
and to find the courage
to ask your name.

Being able to find what
your eyes see,
and your fingers touch,
pale in comparison
to what your mind believes,
your heart feels.

Please don't tell me
that it meant nothing,
for to me
it meant
everything!

You don't find what
we've had just anywhere.
It's something you've
got to have built on,
and lived through.

We've endured many things
since it all started,
kids that have made
their ways in life,
and are starting where
we seem to have left off.

It's not going to be long
before they're living
the dreams we had planned
for them,
and realize the dreams we've
ruined for us.

Right now, we're at a point
to continue moving forward
with what we have,
and put behind the
doubts and lies,
and show each other what
it's like to be trusted,
and safe.

Time will go on,
and our love will wilt away.

I'm sure of this.
I've loved before and lost,
a long time ago,
before there was you.
But I'm willing to give this
another shot
because I know what we've
had in our lives has
made those around us
believe that love can
never die,
and passion would never fade.

So I'll ask you one more time,
just tell me in candor,
what you've got to say,
There is nothing that can
hurt anymore than
knowing what I'm thinking
is the truth.

We've built what we have,
on the trust that we've
found,
in each other,
and that is something
we can both live with
and understand.
I beg of you to
remember this when
your next words flow.

If you want this to end,
tell me a lie again.
But trust me,
with all my love
I know that
it can be repaired
if you're willing

to love me again,
with no strings attached,
no secrets to hide,
and no one to hold your
heart, but I.

My love,
think hard on what you say now,
because all you have,
all I have,
and all we've ever had,
is riding on
one more guess...

Slanted Ship Sunrise, Cancun, Mexico – June 2004